POLAR ANIMAL ADAPTATIONS

by Lisa J. Amstutz

Content Consultant
Jackie Gai, DVM
Zoo and Exotic Animal Consultation

CAPSTONE PRESS
a capstone imprint

A+ Books are published by Capstone Press,
1710 Roe Crest Drive, North Mankato, Minnesota 56003.
www.capstonepub.com

Copyright © 2012 by Capstone Press, a Capstone imprint.
All rights reserved.
No part of this publication may be reproduced in whole or in part, or stored in a retrieval system,
or transmitted in any form or by any means, electronic, mechanical, photocopying, recording,
or otherwise, without written permission of the publisher.
For information regarding permission, write to Capstone Press,
1710 Roe Crest Drive, North Mankato, Minnesota 56003.

Library of Congress Cataloging-in-Publication Data
Amstutz, Lisa J.
 Polar animal adaptations / by Lisa Amstutz.
   p. cm.—(A+ books. Amazing animal adaptations)
 Includes bibliographical references and index.
 Summary: "Simple text and photographs describe polar animal adaptations"—Provided by publisher.
 ISBN 978-1-4296-6031-0 (library binding)—ISBN 978-1-4296-7031-9 (pbk.)
 1. Animals—Polar regions—Juvenile literature. I. Title. II. Series.
 QL104.A67 2012
 591.70911'3—dc22   2011004617

Credits
Jeni Wittrock, editor; Matt Bruning and Gene Bentdahl, designers; Wanda Winch, media
   researcher; Eric Manske, production specialist

Photo Credits
Alamy: Blaine Harrington III, 13, blickwinkel, 22, First Light/Thomas Kitchin & Victoria Hurst, 23; Ardea: Andrey Zvoznikov, 11; DigitalVision, cover, 12; flpa.co.uk: H Hautala, 19; Getty Images Inc: National Geographic/Paul Nicklen, 15, Rick Price, 14, Wayne Lynch, 16-17; iStockphoto: Irving N. Saperstein, 8-9, John Pitcher, 1, Pauline S. Mills, 20, Rich Phalin, 10, Tersina Shieh, 21; Nature Picture Library: Steven Kazlowski, 7; Shutterstock: Armin Rose, 4-5, Arto Hakola, 25, dotweb, 6, file404, cover (design element), FreeSoulProduction, cover (snowflake), kesu, frozen design element, Lily McWilliams, 24, Serg Zastavkin, 18, Sylvie Bouchard, 28, Witold Kaszkin, 26-27

Note to Parents, Teachers, and Librarians
The Amazing Animal Adaptations series uses full color photographs and a nonfiction format to introduce the concept of animal adaptations. *Polar Animal Adaptations* is designed to be read aloud to a pre-reader or to be read independently by an early reader. Photographs help listeners and early readers understand the text and concepts discussed. The book encourages further learning by including the following sections: Table of Contents, Glossary, Read More, Internet Sites, and Index. Early readers may need assistance using these features.

TABLE OF CONTENTS

Life at the Poles.................... 4

What to Wear 6

Polar Body Parts................. 16

Polar Animal Behavior 24

Glossary........................... 30

Read More 31

Internet Sites 31

Index 32

Life at the Poles

The North and South Poles are like giant freezers most of the year. Brrrr!

Polar animals have special ways to stay warm and find food in their snowy homes. We call these ways "adaptations."

What to Wear

Some polar animals wear fur coats to keep warm. A musk ox wears two! The bottom coat is soft and warm. The top coat is shaggy and long.

The arctic fox's coat is the warmest of any mammal. When the fox gets chilly, it sits on its furry tail like a cushion. Then it tucks in its nose to stay warm.

Did you know that polar bears have hollow hair? Tube-shaped fur traps heat in the middle.

All that heat soaks into the bear's black skin. Why black? The dark color is the best at holding in heat.

Snowy owls change colors by the season. Their white winter feathers match snow. Brown summer feathers match plants and rock on the tundra.

One of the owl's prey, the lemming, turns colors too. It changes from brown to white, just like the owl. An adult owl eats up to five lemmings each day—if it can find them!

Penguin chicks have fuzzy down feathers to stay extra warm on land. As the chicks become adults, they grow waterproof feathers to hunt in the icy ocean.

Another bird, the ptarmigan, grows its own fuzzy slippers. Its feathery feet keep it warm when walking on the cold tundra.

How else do polar animals stay warm? Blubber! Ringed seals have a layer of fat, called blubber, under their skin. Blubber keeps the seals warm and helps them float.

A bowhead whale's blubber is about 18 inches (46 centimeters) thick. Bowhead whales live in cold water all year long.

Polar Body Parts

Arctic hares don't need earmuffs to keep their ears warm. Their ears are short and furry. Longer ears would get too cold and suffer frostbite.

Although their ears are short, arctic hares are bigger than other hares. Their large body size holds in heat.

Many polar animals have big feet to help them walk on snow without sinking. A wolverine's big paws act like snowshoes.

A reindeer's wide hooves are also good for walking on snow. More than that, they help the reindeer dig under the snow for food.

Walrus tusks look like giant teeth.
But they aren't made for chewing.

Walruses use their tusks to climb out of the water, chop holes in the ice, and fight.

People put antifreeze in their cars. It keeps the water inside from freezing. Atlantic cod make their own antifreeze. It keeps them from turning into frozen fish sticks in the icy ocean.

22

The wood frog has special blood too. As the frog freezes, its heart and breathing stop. In the spring it thaws out again, good as new.

Polar Animal Behavior

The arctic ground squirrel snoozes through the coldest part of the year. It hibernates for up to eight months. It is one of the few polar animals that hibernates.

Many polar animals migrate to warmer places in winter. The arctic tern flies from the Arctic to the Antarctic each year. Then it flies back. It can fly more than a million miles in its lifetime.

From colored feathers to wide hooves, polar animals are experts at living in the cold. Adaptations help polar animals survive in the icy Arctic and Antarctic areas.

This chart shows polar adaptations mentioned in this book. Can you remember each animal's adaptation?

Animal	Behavior	Body Covering	Body Parts
Arctic fox		●	
Arctic ground squirrel	●		
Arctic hare			●
Arctic tern	●		
Atlantic cod			●
Bowhead whale		●	

Animal	Behavior	Body Covering	Body Parts
Lemming		●	
Musk ox		●	
Penguin		●	
Polar bear		●	
Ptarmigan		●	
Reindeer			●
Ringed seal		●	
Snowy owl		●	
Walrus			●
Wolverine			●
Wood frog			●

29

Glossary

adaptation—a change a living thing goes through to better fit in with its environment

Antarctic—the area near the South Pole

antifreeze—a chemical that is added to a liquid to stop it from freezing

Arctic—the area near the North Pole

blubber—a thick layer of fat under the skin of an animal

down—the soft, fluffy feathers of a bird

frostbite—a condition that occurs when cold temperatures freeze skin

hibernate—to spend the winter in a deep sleep; animals hibernate to survive low temperatures and a lack of food

migrate—to move from one place to another when seasons change or food is scarce

tundra—a flat, cold area without trees; the ground stays frozen in the tundra for most of the year

Read More

Lynette, Rachel. *Who Lives on the Cold, Icy Tundra?* Exploring Habitats. New York: PowerKids Press, 2011.

Salas, Laura Purdie. *Tundras: Frosty, Treeless Lands.* Amazing Science-Ecosystems. Minneapolis: Picture Window Books, 2009.

Underwood, Deborah. *Hiding in the Polar Regions.* Creature Camouflage. Chicago: Heinemann Library, 2011.

Internet Sites

FactHound offers a safe, fun way to find Internet sites related to this book. All of the sites on FactHound have been researched by our staff.

Here's all you do:

Visit *www.facthound.com*

Type in this code: 9781429660310

Check out projects, games and lots more at www.capstonekids.com

Index

arctic fox, 7
arctic ground squirrels, 24
arctic hares, 16
arctic terns, 25
Atlantic cod, 22
blubber, 14, 15
bowhead whales, 15
colors, 9, 10, 11
down, 12
ears, 16, 17
feathers, 10, 12, 26
feet, 13, 18
fur, 6, 7, 8, 16
hibernation, 24
hooves, 19, 26

lemmings, 11
migration, 25
musk oxen, 6
penguins, 12
polar bears, 8–9
ptarmigans, 13
reindeer, 19
ringed seals, 14
snowy owls, 10
tails, 7
tusks, 20–21
walruses, 20–21
wolverines, 18
wood frogs, 23